Surrounded
by His
Grace

Surrounded by His Grace

Embracing the Power of God's Love

By

Michele LaMar-Thomas

SURROUNDED BY HIS GRACE

Embracing the Power of God's Love

ISBN: 979-8-218-64643-1

Printed in the United States of America

My Heart is overflowing with a good theme; I recite my composition concerning the King; My tongue is the pen of a ready writer.

—PSALMS 45:1 (NKJV)

ACKNOWLEDGMENTS

I am deeply grateful to God, whose grace and love continue to inspire and sustain me. This book would not have been possible without His guidance.

To my family and friends—thank you for your unwavering support, encouragement, and prayers. Your love has been a constant source of strength.

A special thanks to my husband, Tony, whose insights, feedback, and belief in this work have meant the world to me.

Finally, to my readers—your time and openness to these words are truly appreciated. May this book bless and uplift you as much as writing it has blessed me.

CONTENTS

PREFACE

The question that has plagued me my entire life is not just why I am here, but what the greater meaning of life is beyond merely living. Surely, God had more in mind when He intricately and uniquely formed each of us in His image. As I reflect on what He wants me to learn during my time on earth—with its highs and lows, agonies and defeats, joys and victories—I am deeply grateful for it all. No, I have not mastered this thing called life, but I am thankful for every moment God has kept me.

Through every challenge and triumph, I feel compelled to share the lessons I've learned about God's grace and mercy—truths that have anchored me through life's uncertainties. This book is the result of that calling. While some of God's intentions are clear to me now, others will only be revealed when I see Him face to face.

In every heartache, disappointment, uncertainty, fear, and victory, one thing remains certain: God has always been with me. And I believe our life lessons are not meant to be kept to ourselves. This book, drawn from personal experiences, is a testament to the goodness of God and an encouragement to its readers. No matter how difficult your current season may be, hold on—trust that God will meet you exactly where you are.

Redemption

Oh death, where is thy sting?

Oh grave, where is thy victory?

—1 CORINTHIANS 15:55 (KJV)

Risen

A kiss seals my fate
Love's betrayal comes swiftly
Yet I rise from death

"I am the true vine, and My Father is the vinedresser."

—JOHN 15:1 (NKJV)

Christ, the Living Vine

A light amidst the darkness
Shines brightly in despair.
God, our blessed Redeemer,
Knows our every care.

Left alone—a lowly branch,
Seeking the Living Vine.
Connected to His power,
Lies victory divine.

"But now, in union with Christ Jesus, you who used to be far away have been brought near by the blood of Christ."

—EPHESIANS 2:13 (GNT)

Brought Near to Christ

Trading beauty for ashes,
Steeped in the Savior's blood,
My will I have abandoned,
Redeemed by His faithful love.
Wonderful Counselor, Redeemer, Friend
He whose love has no end.
Out of the water, I rise brand new,
What He did for me,
He will do for you.

"And the vessel that He made of clay was marred in the hand of the potter; so He made it again into another vessel, as it seemed good to the potter to make."

—JEREMIAH 18:4 (NKJV)

Clay in the Potter's Hand

As I stroll toward the sunlight,
My soul senses His presence
Lifting my hands, I surrender—
Praise to the one true God!

He who heals the brokenhearted,
And makes shattered pieces whole
In His magnificence, I bow low
Yielding like clay in the Potter's hand.

Being molded with care,
Uncertainty and fear dissipate
The Potter breathes in me new life
Revived, life has new meaning.

Reborn, I lift my hands in awe,
Made in His image, I see
My worth for the first time—
Fearfully and wonderfully made.

"Jesus said to her, 'I am the resurrection and the life. He who believes in Me, though he may die, shall live.'"

—JOHN 11:25 (NKJV)

Through Christ's Death, I Live

Crushed for our
unrighteousness, Christ bore
our guilt and shame, securing
our forgiveness, His blood
cleansed every stain.

In triduum and power,
He rose from that now-empty grave,
bringing hope and blessed assurance—
our debts decisively paid.

And so, each Easter Sunday,
we give thanks and praise His name,
glory to God, our Redeemer—
our lives forever changed.

"Lord, you alone are my portion and my cup;
You make my lot secure."

—PSALMS 16:5 (NIV)

In Christ Alone

In Christ alone,
New hope is found.
Jesus Christ,
The sweetest sound.

In power and might,
He ran death aground.
Forever in Christ,
I'm heaven bound.

In His presence,
Joy bells resound.
In Christ alone,
A love profound.

Humility

"The LORD reached down from above and took hold of me; He pulled me out of the deep waters."

—2 SAMUEL 22:17 (GNT)

Upside Down

Oceans
Spinning all around—
Sometimes up
Sometimes down

Drifting
Floating
Upon the seas
Spirit moving
Light and free

Calmness,
Steady over waves
My life once off course
But now am saved.

"But God forbid that I should boast except in the cross of our Lord Jesus Christ."

—GALATIANS 6:14 (NKJV)

Hide Me Behind the Cross

Hide me, Lord, behind the cross,
That pride may find no place.

Let the echoes of my soul
Sing a chorus filled with grace.

Purge my mind of secret faults,
Let no hiding place remain.

Shine Your light in every fold,
Cleanse me from guilt and shame.

Oh, may my life reflect the grace
You offer and so freely bestow.

Sing Glory, Hallelujah!
In Christ alone, I abode

"When I was a child, I spoke and thought and reasoned as a child. But when I grew up, I put away childish things."

—1 CORINTHIANS 13:11 (NLT)

putting away childish things

yesterday, I was a child, i spoke,
understood, and reasoned as one—
lacking wisdom, in need of discipline.

today, no longer simpleminded,
i place naïve logic in a giveaway
bag, like clothes that no longer fit.

my heart's barrenness, once pronounced,
has found the answer to my existence.
a heavy load is lifted, freeing my spirit to soar.

for me, living is Christ, so I rise,
above and beyond life's uncertainties,
i press on to lay hold of that
which lasts for eternity.

"Therefore, do not be unwise, but understand what the will of the Lord is."

—EPHESIANS 5:17 (NKJV)

A Prayer Seeking God's Will

Seeking Your thoughts toward me,
I enter Your courts with praise.
Humbly, I bow before You,
Recalling Your merciful ways.

Resting in full assurance,
You hear me when I pray.
Lord, keep my heart from pretense,
Spirit order my steps in your way.

Uphold me in your presence,
Lest I should go astray.
I lift my longing soul in awe
Lead me through each day.

*"He heals the brokenhearted and binds
up their wounds."*

—PSALMS 147:3 (NKJV)

Tell God

Tell God all your trials,
Cast on Him your cares.
In the lowest valley,
He will meet you there.

There is not a problem
He can't see you through.
Take a chance on Jesus—
It's up to you to choose.

Tomorrow is not promised,
Don't let this day slip past .
Give your life to Jesus,
Let Him redeem your past.

*"Surely there is a future, and your
hope will not be cut off."*

—PROVERBS 23:18 (NIV)

There Is Hope for You

You started out strong,
A heart willing to do its part
Right now, hiding in the dark

Playing games and acting insane,
Chasing thing which will not remain
Return to Jesus—Come just as you are

He will heal your hurts,
Mend every scar
Hold you close in loving arms

"But thank God! He gives us victory over sin and death through our Lord Jesus Christ."

—1 CORINTHIANS 15:57 (NLT)

The Difference Maker

Knowing Christ has made
All the difference in my life
Having once searched the world over
Placing my hope on a four-leaf clover
I was wandering, void of care
All the while, my Savior near
Without warning a light appeared
Chancing an untrodden path
His counsel laid hold of my fear
A new birth, a changed name,
My life is forever secure.
This old self, hidden in Christ
Has made all the difference in my life.

God's Love

"At noon, darkness fell across the whole land until three o'clock."

—MATTHEW 27:45 (NLT)

No Ordinary Day

It was no ordinary day,
On a hill far away,
Jesus, our Messiah, was slain.

Betrayed by a kiss,
Yet He did not resist—
For the apostate, no redemption remained.

Innocence hung on the cross,
All hope seemed lost,
In a borrowed tomb the Savior was laid.

Then, on the third day,
With the stone rolled away,
Christ rose in power—mighty to save.

"I do everything to spread the Good News and share in its blessings."

—1 CORINTHIANS 9:23 (NLT)

The Question Is

Where in the dark
will your light shine
how will the world
know you are Mine?

Will your light flicker
beneath a small tree,
or stretch across rooftops
for the world to see?

Where in the dark
will your light shine
how will they know
I am the Christ Divine?

"When you go through the waters, I will be with you. When you go through rivers of difficulty, you will not drown."

—ISAIAH 43:2 (NLT)

God's Faithful Love

God looked upon my brokenness,
Observing the worst in me.

Struggling in the deepest of waters,
With compassion, He rescued me.

Evermore your steadfast love I proclaim,
My will I surrender to Thee.

Now my heart knows Redemption's song—
To my God, I eternally cling.

"I will search for my lost ones who strayed away, and I will bring them safely home again."

—EZEKIEL 34:16 (NLT)

You Kept Calling Me

You kept calling, despite knowing where I'd been
My life was destitute mired in sin
Hopeless, downcast, and without a friend

Alone in my despair,
I cried, Lords, Here I am!
Taking my hand, you drew me in.

How do I speak of love given freely
Where do I begin?
Praise to the God who know me when

Glory to God, who has broken every chain.
You cast off my darkness, my sorrow, my shame.
You never stopped calling me by name,

Glory Hallelujah Amen.

"Give thanks to the Lord of Lords. His faithful love endures forever."

—PSALMS 136:3 (NLT)

My Help Comes from the Lord

Your strong love
Lit the darkness within.

The way out was hard to see, No hope of a life lived free.

In the depths of despair,
You restored my hope.

Who would have imagined
My life—vibrant and full.

The sting of death curbed,
I am so loved.

Now, able to love in return—
A lesson from God,
A redemption unearned.

Faith

"We know how much God loves us, and we have put our trust in His love."

—1 JOHN 4:16 (NLT)

Trust in God

Weary, upside down,
Gaze upon God for support,
Take hold of His peace.

Rise with assurance,
For He knows the path you take.
Let love guide the way.

"You will keep him in perfect peace, whose mind is stayed on You, because he trusts in You."

—ISAIAH 26:3 (NKJV)

Perfect Peace

Lord, let my life reflect Your peace,
Like a flower—unrestrained,
Braving shifting winds of change,
Disrobed and unashamed.

"Trust in Him at all times, you people; pour out your hearts to him, for God is our refuge."

—PSALMS 62:8 (NIV)

The Choice

Life is never smoothly paved,
Oft strewn with rocks along the way
Yet among them, joy remains—
Sunshine, laughter, peace of mind
I would not ask to trade one for the other
For in these moments, virtue is garnered
But one choice we each must make
Chose to stumble through life or be guided by grace
It is in His hands, I place my faith
For my God knows the road I take.

"And after the earthquake a fire, but the LORD was not in the fire; and after the fire a still small voice."

—1 KINGS 19:12 (KJV)

A Still Small Voice

A still small voice,
echoes in the wind,
beckoning steadily,
come on in.

Will you answer,
or turn away once more—
the one your heart Is
yearning for?

Waiting patiently,
God stands aside,
longing to hold you,
free you from pride.

He holds the answers,
to all our life's struggles,
run to meet Him,
bow down, humble.

It's not too late,
no need to hesitate,
come—lest the night
seal your fate.

"Thou art my hiding place and my shield: I hope in Thy Word."

—PSALM 119:114

The Hiding Place

What am I in this grand orb of life,
and to whom shall I make my plea?

I sit, picking my sores, waiting
for the Balm of Gilead to heal these wounds.

In my distress, I called to the Lord Most High,
and he hearkened to me from Heaven's throne.

Whispering do not fear, for I see your tears,
take shelter in the shadow of my wings.

For I alone am your hiding place,
and carry you through the storms of life.

There you will find hope in trouble
in me, healing for your soul.

Healing

"A cheerful heart is good medicine, but a broken spirit saps a person's strength."

—PROVERBS 17:22 (NLT)

Laughter Is Good Medicine

Just like medicine
Laughter soothes the soul
Chasing away the blues

"Their seeds produced plants and trees of the same kind. And God saw that it was good."

—GENESIS 1:12B (NLT)

Bold and Beautiful

Embraced by the sun
Wildflowers dance in meadows
Unburdened by shame

"Sing a new song to the Lord, for He has done wonderful deeds."

—PSALMS 98:1 (NLT)

Sing a New Song

Awakened by the sounds of dawn,
little birdies chirp through an open
window.

A melody of light,
the starry night has taken flight,
praise God for a brand-new day.

Wiping cobwebs from my eyes—
from the warm bed, I rise,
joyful for all a new day brings.

With both feet on the ground,
alive here and now,
I join in on the song the birdies sing.

As I choose to leave the past behind,
nothing's going to slow me down,
going to let my little light shine.

"And if it seem evil to you to serve the LORD, choose you this day whom you will serve."

—JOSHUA 24:15 (KJV)

Chose Life

She rises, excited about the day,
refusing to give in to the "what ifs"
that rankle in her mind.

No, today will be different.
It is the day of her breakthrough.
Bending her knees in hope
of the promise not yet realized,
she is unburdened by fear.

Fore, she deems He who has
promised will not forsake her.
because of God's past faithfulness
she refuses to live caught between two opinions
and has chosen this day, whom she will serve.

*"He heals the brokenhearted
and binds up their wounds."*

—PSALMS 147:3 (NKJV)

Mender of Hearts

Hiding from outside chatter
My spirit sinks quite low
Lost in unyielding sadness
Ebbing in unyielding sorrow.

Alarmed by the yoke of self-pity
I climb back from my despair
Resting in contemplation, I remember
God has always been there
The Mender of broken hearts

It was not for naught He surrendered
Giving His life for you and for me
When this ole life is over
With God, I'll eternally be

Shown love forgiving and tender,
I press on in power to live free
Glory to God in the highest
The Mender of broken hearts

Praise and Thanksgiving

"Thanks be to God for His indescribable gift!"

—2 CORINTHIANS 9:15 (NKJV)

I Live to Give Thanks

The Savior's love flows deep within,
And by His blood, I'm cleansed.

I cannot explain it at all— Tell
me, where would I begin?

One thing I know for certain, Jesus calls me friend.

Once lost, trapped in a bottomless pit,
His love lifted me to higher ground.

No way to repay the debt I owe,
Set free from the past, no burden to tow.

New life imparted graciously,
A promise kept so faithfully.

Glory to the one true God—
Forever grateful, humbly I trod.

"But He was wounded for our transgressions, He was bruised for our iniquities.
The chastisement for our peace was upon Him, and by His stripes we are healed."

—ISAIAH 53:5 (NKJV)

The Promise of the Cross

Descending from Heaven's throne,
Christ bore our guilt and shame.
His blood spilled for our redemption—
My life forever changed.

The stone rolled away in victory,
The sting of death erased.
Communion with God restored,
The promise of the Cross fulfilled.

Nestled safely in the Savior's arms,
Despair takes wings and flees.
My heart bursts forth in song,
Praising God to heavenly heights.

"Don't brag about tomorrow, since you don't know what a day will bring."

—PROVERBS 27:1 (NLT)

This Day I Live

You never know what a day will bring,
I've often heard it said.
So why boast about tomorrow?
Cherish each moment instead.

For tomorrow has yet to come,
By the Spirit's power, be led.
Take time to smell the roses,
Give thanks for opened eyes.

Sing Glory, Hallelujah!
Let your life and light shine.
You never know what a day will bring—
Now's the opportunity to thrive.

"Give thanks unto the Lord, for he is good; his love endures forever."

—PSALM 118:1 (NIV)

Jesus

J – Jewels that shine in our Savior's crown.

E – Emancipation for those once bound.

S – Salvation freely given, bringing release.

U – United, His disciples rise for the world to see.

S – Surrendered to His Word and His ways.

"Now I stand on solid ground, and I will publicly praise the Lord."

—PSALMS 26:12 (NLT)

Amazing Grace

I often sit in wonder, God,
At the grace You've shown to me.
My heart bursts with thankfulness,
Assured in You, I am free.

Unmerited favor from above,
bestowed in vast amounts.
You extinguish all my fears,
Erasing all my doubts.

My soul overflows in praise, From this unworthy fount.
I lift my voice in joyful song,
For sacrifice made on my account.

God may my life reflect Your mercy,
To those still bound and without.
Let it shine with overflowing love,
Showing what life in Christ is about.

"You will show me the path of life; in Your presence there is fullness of joy."

—PSALMS 16:11 (NKJV)

Alone in His Presence

Lord, in your presence,
I yearn to be.
It's there your Spirit
speaks to me.

In the stillness of serene nights,
My heart seeks a guiding light.
Father, reveal the road I take—

Let me not err,
Nor succumb to pride.
Your will, not mine
I humbly abide.

Eternal Peace

"A highway shall be there, and a road, and it shall be called the Highway of Holiness."

—ISAIAH 35:8 (NKJV)

Heaven

Majestic are the stars that shine,
Lighting the way to Heaven's gate.
One day, I'll travel along its path,
Casting off remnants of all that was.

I'll depart this world for home,
Taking my place in eternity—
Where peace flows like a river,
And suffering and sorrow cease.

"For I know that my Redeemer lives, and He shall stand at last on the earth."

—JOB 19:25 (NKJV)

My Lifeline Divine

I made it through,
Holding onto You— Jesus,
my lifeline divine.

The source of light,
Shining forever bright—
Jesus, my lifeline divine.

You covered my sin,
Giving me hope within—
Jesus, my lifeline divine.

Blessings from above,
Oh, forever I'm loved—
Jesus, my lifeline divine.

"But who can endure the day of His coming, and who can stand when He appears? For He is like a refiner's fire and like fullers' soap."

—MALACHI 3:2 (ESV)

The King Is Coming

The King is coming,
With a righteous arm,
Wielding a swift sword,
Showing Himself strong.

Bringing perfect justice,
Righting every wrong,
All will bow before Him,
The redeemed shall sing a new song.

Christ our Lord is coming,
To reign upon His throne.
Lift every voice in symphony,
In praise of Christ alone.

"And as God's grace reaches more and more people, there will be greater thanksgiving, and God will receive more and more glory."

—2 CORINTHIANS 4:15 (NLT)

Surrounded by God's Grace

On the glorious side of Heaven,
We'll meet face to face.
Tell the story of two strangers,
Bound by God's amazing grace.

I never would have made it,
All alone and without faith.
It was God who sent an angel,
To tell me of His grace.

As I began to listen,
My life began to change.
Today, I count the ways
That I am not the same.

Of the things I've learned,
Indeed, God's love is true.
He gave me a brand-new life,
He can do the same for you.

Special Dedication

"For now, we see in a mirror dimly but then face to face. Now I know in part, but then I shall know just as I am known."

—1 CORINTHIANS 13:12 (NKJV)

Edna Mae

I never knew my grandmother, on
my father's side. When Dad was
just a toddler, she went to her
home on high.

Many say I look like her— Edna
Mae was her name.

Would I have called her grandma?
Did she have a favorite rhyme?
Was her favorite color blue, like mine?

Perhaps she loved the winter's frost
more than summer's golden shine.
I wonder.

Staring at her portrait,
her eyes—lovely, inviting,
and kind. A smile as radiant as the sun, Lips
the color of wine.

I would have loved her instantly; My
heart feels it deep inside.
Gazing upon her portrait
fills me with a sense of pride.

In these tranquil
ponderings, my questions
put to rest, I feel so very
blessed.

Children's Children are the crown of old men,
And the glory of children is their father.

—PROVERBS 17:6 (NLT)

A Father's Legacy

Dad taught me to ride a bike,
And I don't mean just any trike— A
ruby-red racer with a horn to blow,
Its frame sparkling in sunlight's glow.

A brave girl, so here was the deal:
We had to get rid of those training wheels.
Dad said, "Okay, but let's take it slow."
Both hands on that bike, I was ready to go!

Running beside me, his hand on the fender, Dad's
steady guidance is what I remember.
And then came the time I crashed into a wall— But
I had nothing to fear; Dad didn't let me fall.

Now, today, at sixty-six
Guess who's the reason I still love to ride?
Fearless of twists, bends in the road and all— Cause
Dad taught me to ride when I was small.

ABOUT THE AUTHOR

Michele LaMar-Thomas writes poetry that touches on the human experience, such as faith, love, struggle, redemption, and victory. Writing a book was always on her bucket list, and eventually, with Brown Girl Rising: A Poetry Memoir, it became a reality. Surrounded by His Grace: Embracing the Power of God's Love is her second book.

A recently retired public school teacher with a Master's in TESOL, Michele enjoys her time as a caregiver. When not writing, she loves spending time with family, volunteering at the community food bank, church ministry, and traveling. She lives in Ohio with her devoted husband of thirty-five years.